Courage Beyond Fear

Courage Beyond Fear

Re-Formation in Theological Education

EDITED BY

Katie Day

AND

Deirdre Good

FOREWORD BY

Milton McC. Gatch

PICKWICK *Publications* · Eugene, Oregon

COURAGE BEYOND FEAR
Re-Formation in Theological Education

Pickwick Publications
An Imprint of Wipf and Stock Publishers
199 W. 8th Ave., Suite 3
Eugene, OR 97401

www.wipfandstock.com

PAPERBACK ISBN: 978-1-5326-4708-6
HARDCOVER ISBN: 978-1-5326-6130-3
EBOOK ISBN: 978-1-5326-6131-0

Cataloguing-in-Publication data:

Names: Day, Katie, editor. | Good, Deirdre, editor

Title: Courage beyond fear : re-formation in theological education / edited by Katie Day and Deirdre Good.

Description: Eugene, OR: Pickwick Publications, 2019 | Includes bibliographical references.

Identifiers: ISBN 978-1-5326-4708-6 (paperback) | ISBN 978-1-5326-6130-3 (hardcover) | ISBN 978-1-5326-6131-0 (ebook)

Subjects: LCSH: Religious education. | Theology—Study and teaching. | Protestant theological seminaries

Classification: CC BV4070 C58 2019 (print) | LCC BV4070 (ebook)

Manufactured in the U.S.A.   01/16/19

Dedicated to our co-laborers in the vineyard of theological education, whose witness to the truth of God's word will survive and transform institutions.

Contents

Chapter 4: Marginalization

Chapter 5: Power in Community

Chapter 6: Forgiveness

Acknowledgments

WITHOUT THE GENEROSITY AND stamina of spouses, friends, students, colleagues past and present, and strangers who took the time to send emails and letters of support, this book would not exist. In particular we would like to thank Bishop Fred Borsch, mentor and friend to us both (and to many readers), whose death we continue to mourn.

Foreword

MILTON McC. GATCH, PhD

Emeritus, Union Theological Seminary

CHRISTIANITY IS BASED IN a yearning for change: for the perfection of creation in the Kingdom of God, which we are assured by the resurrection must come to fruition, transforming our imperfect selves and our imperfect cosmos, in God's own time. In our daily lives, we also seek change to make things better: change of ourselves, of our institutions, of our country. Change wrought by human agency can sometimes improve persons or institutions, but it can also undermine what is or was good. The prime example of destructive change in our time is the disruption of climate and ecology by human agency, which threatens the very viability of "this fragile earth, our island home." Often religious groups have the temerity to claim that change sought or being implemented is carrying out the will of God—a claim that is, quite simply, blasphemous.

Theological education—the enterprise that educates and trains women and men to minister in religious institutions or to carry theological insight into other activities in the world—is in a perilous state. Many denominations are shrinking, financial support is dwindling, and small theological schools serving denominations are expensive and poorly supported. Controversies rage over how to adapt to the difficulties of the present, how to make enfeebled institutions healthy, prosperous, and responsive to the religious mission in the present century. Institutions have seen no recourse but to merge, to close, or to experiment with a "new vision" that upends a heritage developed and treasured for a century or more.

Often in these situations, the administration and faculties of theological schools (and not only seminaries) cannot find a workable solution to the dilemma, and governing boards step in with what they regard as either visionary or tough-minded solutions. They may go outside the circle of theological education to recruit presidents or deans who lack experience of and respect for academic tradition, not to mention the customary credentials of educational leadership. They may decide that they do not have adequate resources to continue and must close the institution, sending students off elsewhere and putting the faculty on the street (with what is said to be generous and adequate terminal compensation). They may move or give what is left in capital resources and books to another, apparently stronger, institution. They may remove faculty and institute a radical reorientation in which the participation of faculty and students in governance is radically diminished, standards for faculty recruitment are lowered, and curricular development is arrogated to administration and the board. Consensus seems rarely, if ever, to be an operative consideration.

Whatever the particular situation of a seminary in crisis, change in these situations is painful and destructive. This book collects sermons or addresses given by students and faculty members of institutions in crisis at moments of radical change. These discourses are marked by pain—excruciating professional, personal, and spiritual pain. Yet they are remarkable to me for the absence of vitriol in the face of great personal and professional suffering; for the prevalence of profound reflection on the nature and practice of forgiveness; and for their indirection: under constraint not to name the seminary crisis, they let racism, passive resistance, reaction to pandemic disease, and response to the attacks of September 11, 2001, serve as apt metaphors. In their forbearance and indirection, they find deeper truth than a recitation of grievances could convey.

This book, so aptly named *Courage Beyond Fear*, teaches us about wise, faithful, and forgiving bravery in the face of personal suffering and institutional dislocation. What it does not and cannot do is what must now be our task: to reimagine a theological education that rests on the great traditions of Christian learning, practice, and pastoral care and simultaneously confronts the challenges of this troubled time.

Introduction

KATIE DAY AND DEIRDRE GOOD

FIVE SEMINARY PROFESSORS, SOME in clerical collars, stood on the sidewalk outside the offices of a legal firm. As they were getting ready to go inside, a passing cyclist spotted them and shouted out: "Are you the fired seminary faculty?" They assented, and the bicyclist continued, "The church fired me too! Good luck!"

How did we get there? Take any theological school with long-standing financial problems (not insurmountable on their own) and hire unqualified administrators with questionable interpersonal skills and a mandate to turn things around, who then clash with some or all of the faculty. Add a board that doesn't understand (or in some cases, care about) theological education and is filled with nice church people who can't handle conflict. What happens next is a crisis that is being played out in theological schools and seminaries across this country.

Why should you care? Maybe it's a good thing that places where people train to be priests, pastors, and church leaders are downsizing or closing, particularly if so-called Christian denominations are losing members and local churches cannot support anything more than even one part-time clergy position. Aren't people voting with their feet, indicating that the "old line" denominations just aren't meeting their individual or social needs?

Here's why these crises matter to a broader public beyond people who wish to self-identify as religious. In our present world we need people to think deeply in community about profound and ultimate questions like the meaning of life and human longing for

1

God in places that are not driven solely by issues of financial expediency. The forms of religious leadership might be changing, but the need for spiritual insight and community are not.

At the same time, we need people who want to engage in this strange and brilliant activity to not have to graduate from seminaries with mountains of debt. And it turns out, in a weird and wonderful way, that living through crises connects to a search for meaning; shining through the debris and fissures of institutional catastrophes are shards of insight and fragments of hope shared in community that offer insights into issues at stake as well as contours of the changing landscape of theological education.

This book shares some of these insights in order to provide reflections and resources that support people trying to survive institutional crises with integrity. Leaders can implement drastic changes resulting in organizational crises not just in theological seminaries and divinity schools. Anyone experiencing authoritarian (or "disruptive") leadership will recognize what we have lived through and recognize our attempts to understand and respond to our situations.

Material in this book stands as a record of a particular time and place. This record needs to be in the public domain as a reflection of truths of particular seminary communities inhabited and embodied by their faculty, staff, and students because that history and those realities are in danger of being obliterated from public accounts of seminary history. In a post-truth era, in which alternative facts attempt to erase not just present reality but the very construction of that reality, we need to keep alive voices of all constituencies, past and present. Precisely because many of us have left, or have been forced to leave these institutions, we need to make sure that these voices are not erased from a construction of the history of our seminaries that is simply untrue. Indeed, to refuse to hear or think through implications of the words spoken through this book is to shore up an alternative reality that masquerades as theological education. We cannot allow alternative facts to replace reality.

Background

We know through media and press releases that today many seminaries and places of theological education are experiencing and have been going through crises for several decades as denominational affiliations decrease, student enrollment drops, and funding diminishes. Some institutions like Bangor Theological Seminary in Bangor and Portland, Maine, have closed. Against the backdrop of decreasing enrollments and financial stringency, others are merging: Andover Newton Theological School, the oldest theological graduate institution in the nation, has closed its campus in Newton, Massachusetts, and relocated to Yale Divinity School; three Assemblies of God institutions voted to consolidate in Springfield, Missouri, in 2011; the Jesuit School of Theology merged with Santa Clara University in California in 2009; the Lutheran Theological Seminary at Gettysburg, Pennsylvania, has moved to unite with the Lutheran Theological Seminary at Philadelphia; and the Board of Episcopal Divinity School in Cambridge, Massachusetts, voted to merge with Union Theological Seminary in New York City.

An accrediting agency for theological institutions, the Association for Theological Schools, notes that enrollment at its member schools has been on a steady decline for decades: total head count at member institutions in the United States and Canada fell from 74,253 in 2011 to 71,950 in 2014 and 72,116 in 2015. Simultaneously, member schools are growing from 260 in 2011 to 272 in 2015 but these are the smallest schools with fewer than 75 students enrolled. For example, America Evangelical University, a forty-six-student institution in Los Angeles affiliated with the Korean Evangelical Holiness Church, received Association of Theological Schools associate membership in 2014. China Evangelical Seminary North America, a fifty-six-student nondenominational institution in West Covina, California, received accreditation in 2015. Midsize schools with between 151 and 1,000 students either have flat enrollments or are decreasing in size.

But what is it really like for employees and students at these institutions to go through changes? Press releases and official statements about closings, changes, and mergers do not describe the lived reality of students, staff, and faculty. Further, affected groups often do not want to "go public" out of loyalty to their schools or wanting to protect a possible position in the new institution. This book does just that by listening to and reading between the lines of meditations, reflections, and sermons of students, staff, and faculty given in the midst of crises during community gatherings, particularly worship. While statistics like those above are available to describe the changes, theological interpretations of them have not been widely shared beyond inside circles of those present. Nobody disputes that change is part and parcel of theological education these days and that it presents challenges and opportunities. But internal reflections on transitions like closings, downsizings, and mergers, their human costs, and what they might mean from a spiritual or religious point of view is unacknowledged and undocumented. Further, these religious institutions are modeling leadership for the emerging leaders they are forming—too often, there is a disconnect in the ecclesiology we teach and the corporate style being implemented.

To understand these meditations and sermons, it helps to know the contexts in which they were shared. Worship in seminaries generally includes spoken reflections on Scripture often written in advance. What makes these particular talks striking is that through their focus on sacred Scripture, we can see that each one reflects on some aspect of the crises so as to promote deeper reflection and resolve. Yes, they are theological statements in themselves deliberating on a particular crisis, but they are also part of a wider conversation about meanings of closure and change.

Religious patterns of believing and belonging have been changing, especially in the last decade, but the ramifications have not been fully explored. So, with fewer people in the pews, and consequently decreased mission budgets, what has this meant for institutional structures such as denominations and seminaries? This book focuses particularly on upheaval in theological education and the human costs as well as the theological issues it raises. It is a book written by those who deeply love the church, are committed to its transformation, yet directly impacted by restructuring.

The aim of this book, *Courage Beyond Fear: Re-Formation in Theological Education*, is to understand and interpret actual crises we have survived in theological institutions. Every contributor has experienced first-hand a crisis in the seminary or theological school in which we work(ed). Some continue to work in a changed institution while others left, resigned, or were fired. We first document responses of resistance to authoritarian structures in student and faculty theological meditations and sermons spoken publicly during the institutional upheavals. Then through them we identify dispositions in community crises: shock, staying and witnessing, flight or fight, marginalization, power in community, and forgiveness. Behind these dispositions we identify strategies: opposition without rancor, shared authority, vulnerability and truth telling, hope without expectation, courage beyond fear, and humility without humiliation. The book proposes that these strategies of formation and resistance can be deployed in other authoritarian and paternalistic contexts.

Finally, as the institutional church moves into an uncertain future, these theological reflections from the perspective of those in the midst of institutional transition serve as a resource for the whole church going forward. The challenges of judicatories and educational institutions of the church serve as models of organizational transformation, for better or worse. How do they model leadership and strategic change for the church at this critical moment in its history? What can the church learn from the human experiences of those on the front lines of change?

This book will provide a resource for the whole church to reflect critically on its mission in light of necessary institutional changes. How does the church reflect its Gospel values even as it is in the midst of institutional change? These reflections represent a contribution to the collective wisdom much needed at this point in the history of the church.

Themes in Responses to Crises

Shock

Even with knowledge of likely changes in seminaries and divinity schools due to decreasing enrollment and finances, individual institutions, administrations, and boards respond differently to crises. There may be a thousand tiny shocks over periods of time or several large ones. The degree of the shock depends on the level of knowledge community members have about the state of things and remedies proposed and the meaning of transparency in church leadership. If deliberations on remedies are not public, or not shared in detail, then changes and downsizing come across as sudden surprises. Seminary student Cristi Chapman's sermon describes one crisis in which eight faculty were terminated by the board as an act of robbery. And in the immediate aftermath of being told that administrative changes mean "God is doing a new thing," Paul Rajashekar's reflection points out that God doesn't obliterate the past to create something new. Storm Swain helpfully outlines complications of grief in a seminary change or closure.

Staying and Witnessing

After initial shocks, those continuing in the community experience ongoing catastrophe as both passive receivers and interpreters of the situation. As witnesses, their experience and understanding moves beyond testimony to include hope: maybe someone someday will make better sense of what happened both for those who lived through the present crisis and for those who seek to understand it.

An experience of witnessing crisis in community is not passive. No faculty member in a faculty meeting can read unemotionally an email received from the Board of Trustees chair informing each of us that our (untendered) resignations have been accepted. Accordingly, meditations in this book spoken in community express shock, deep grief, loss, and anger of the whole.

If meditations express a hope that future interpreters will make better sense of the present, they are also ways of inviting outside, even numinous witnesses into the present crisis to address it in some way. Andrew Irving's sermon, "God at the Site of Trauma," points out city spaces and architecture in Berlin and New York testifying to a past cataclysm, or street shrines where candles and flowers witness to a death or accident in a specific spot. At these locations people have stood and continue to stand together, in some cases annually, so as to remember the meaning of places where injuries were sustained and lives were lost. In these ways we seek to make sense of humiliation and death in the context of a religious tradition that affirms God as a humiliated and slaughtered human being active in human history, specifically at sites of trauma, and whose subsequent death and resurrected life embraces and transforms human experiences of anguish and loss.

In a community crisis, everyone struggles to speak about what it means. Some public articulations fall short: we heard sermons from visiting bishops and priests that were brave but ultimately futile efforts to tell everyone that everything will be fine, that we all have scarring moments, and that (addressing students) this crisis will be yours. Other private reflections and conversations, some of which are shared here, exhibit more resilient understandings of crises leading to deeper bonds of affection. Without these supportive communities in which we labored together to speak on how we might conduct ourselves, no one's sanity would have remained intact.

Deirdre Good's reflection asks what it meant to stay through a life-threatening epidemic of yellow fever as Episcopal nuns, African-Americans, and others did in 1878, while ministers and politicians left town. In reflecting on the meaning of such choices we are asking: do you leave your people to die or do you stay and witness and help?

David Hurd reflects in the midst of upheaval on the gift of time to expose multiple layers of a seminary story. He describes a place of theological education as a dwelling where we are staff, teachers, and students together; in which we seek wisdom, even the Way of Wisdom. Folly or foolishness are seen as the opposite of wisdom by St. Paul in his letter to the Corinthians. "But how," he asks, "will we rate our success? Can wisdom or ministry any more be a product than the church itself can be a business, without suffering the corruptions of commerce and politics?"

Flight or Fight

Flight is a natural human response to catastrophe and many in our communities left them for very good reasons. Some needed to continue their education or employment elsewhere and other institutions offered them opportunities to do so in schools not embroiled in crisis. Some took advantage of the occasion of a crisis to move back home to families from whom they had been separated.

Some of us do not have an option to leave: perhaps we are employed by the school and must stay through everything or perhaps other reasons compel us to stay. Perhaps we have ties to the neighborhood and towns or city around it. Perhaps the religious official who will ordain us to ministry or priesthood prefers that we stay. Being present means being there for the duration and having to try to understand its context. In this regard, religious truths can be helpful. After all, several religious traditions including Christianity have at their core an understanding of presence exactly at the point of the most confusion and the most pain. The sermon, "God Is Not a Microwave," by Hershey Mallette Stephens, delivered around the time of her seminary graduation makes the point that in God's time, things happen slowly and for a reason, even through confusion and change. If God's creation of the world takes seven days, and if discernment of our vocations takes time, it is time spent in refusing to skate over and ignore experiences but in drilling down to an understanding that deep meaning can be wrought from pain, hurts, and even unnecessary suffering. This is not masochism. It is careful attention to agonizing events and deep wounds that need to be lived, unpacked, and felt through our bodies before any steps toward healing and wholeness can begin.

It is a time to weep together and a time to minister to each other in the midst of hurt and grief.

Marginalization

At the heart of every educational institution lies a healthy educational experience. In the case of theological education, formation for lay or ordained ministry shapes theological training. Formation is a training of character and virtue in community, focusing on theological instruction rooted in places of God's activity in the world and in faith communities. Thus, every place and each interaction creating and promoting education is central: classrooms, libraries, dining halls, and spaces where people congregate, especially places of worship, and particularly chapel. Yet education is more than being in particular places; it is about cultivating an ethos of learning at the heart of a community, occurring equally well outside and inside classrooms. When intensifying concerns about diminished funding, decreased enrollments, and denominational attrition overtakes that ethos, institutional catastrophes undermine learning everywhere.

Responsibility for an institution usually belongs to the Board of Trustees. Their fiduciary duty is to set the overall direction of the institution, to raise funds, and to guide the administration and faculty in reaching institutional goals. Fiscal responsibility comes first and integrity and mission of the institution follow. To do its job the board needs independent, diligent trustees, willing to apply the statutes and challenge recommendations that come to them. They must also be receptive to all constituent stakeholders.

Already a reality for the majority of those who teach at US colleges and universities, seminary and theological school boards and administrations have increasingly begun to adopt aspects of business models in pursuit of fiscal stability. In academic employment, for example, business models have come to exercise control over working conditions and appointment status of faculty and staff. When trustees make decisions for the institution without attending first to the educational mission of the schools and in consultation with faculty and students, the potential for crisis is great. Employees in these situations find themselves marginalized. In authoritarian institutions, faculty are expected to be docile and obedient. On one occasion we were told by an external visitor to obey the dean and president as one would the captain of the Titanic, issuing orders on a sinking ship. The sermon by Drew Kadel proposes that white faculty in institutional crises, finding themselves now ignored and disregarded, might be in a better position to understand racism.

Power in Community

In teaching people how to live with one another in order to be the kind of community that exhibits the character of the God who called them out of slavery in Egypt, Josh Davis explores Jesus' command to "love your enemies" as a call to embody trust not hostile reactivity. Give and don't ask to be repaid. Seize the initiative and overcome evil with good. This is the humility and vulnerability of true power in community.

Amy Lamborn's sermon seeks to understand deeper aspects of the life of Florence Lee Tim Oi, the first woman ordained to the priesthood in the Anglican Church in 1944. What was the real cost to Florence Lee Tim Oi (and others who supported her) when she was required to renounce her priesthood by her Bishop? When church leaders prize unity and compromise over a prophetic act done in a specific situation, the human cost can be grave.

Forgiveness

Community members can choose to move from being passive recipients of a crisis to reclaim agency within it. We know that there is no future without forgiveness as Archbishop Desmond Tutu says. He also says that forgiveness is letting go of the right to retribution. Thomas Oord, who was laid off in 2015 as a tenured professor of theology, came to propose forgiving those in charge who fired him. Forgiveness, he says, "is a form of love that means intentionally acting to do good to those who have harmed us. It usually involves a pardoning statement of some kind and subsequent actions that treat well or wish wellness to those who have treated us poorly. It also typically involves a long road to change negative emotions to positive ones." This is very hard work.

Conclusion

Each of these sermons and reflections comes from human hearts torn open in public crises of theological institutions. If they express raw searing truths of downsizings, mergers, and closures, they also witness a way forward through grace and hope in community.

1 ————————————————————

Shock

Morning Prayer, Luke 9:51–62

THE REVEREND CRISTI CHAPMAN

Saint Mark's Cathedral, Seattle, Washington
(Homily delivered October 20, 2014)

THIS MORNING, I HOPE to preach the gospel as faithfully as I can in this moment to this community. This chapel is sacred space, not a battleground, not the senate floor, not a pressroom. This chapel is also space where the difficult, countercultural message of the Gospel *must* be proclaimed by each of us without fear and without delay.

[Please pray with me—Gracious and Holy One, we give you thanks for this day, for adding it to our lives and to the lives of those we encounter this day. May God give us ears to hear wisdom in this moment, and voices and actions to proclaim your Good News. Amen.]

On Tuesday, my home in Seattle was robbed.

We don't know who the intruder was. Probably someone trying to feed an addictive drug habit. Someone hurting and on the edge. The thief was looking for change, jewelry, pain killers, Sudafed. The thief stole almost nothing of physical value. What was stolen is irreplaceable—the sense of security and safety of my house sitters, my neighbors, and of my family.

On Friday, my seminary, our seminary, was robbed.

Unlike the robbery on Tuesday, we know exactly who the culprits were . . . those charged with stewarding and shepherding the mission of this place, of our education, and of the future of God's church. The leaders of this place stole the heart of this institution on Friday. They robbed us of the expectation that we, the students of this seminary, study with and be formed by great, world-class scholars.

They disrupted our educations, disrupted our calls to ministry, and for at least a few in this community, they disrupted a fledgling hope in faith. What they took is also irreplaceable.

At a preaching conference in March in Seattle, I heard one of the more profound statements I've heard in a long time. Marcus Borg, Walter Brueggemann, and Lauren Winner had come to stir up the preachers and people of the Diocese of Olympia. One of them said that faithful preachers of the Gospel must realize what a key point of the Gospel is—to call out the dominant power systems that oppress and enslave God's people. Those same preachers must then warn the faithful that those same dominant systems will do everything in their power possible to squash and kill any attempt to overthrow their grasp on power. Jesus tried to find another way. As his followers, we, too, must find another way. God's kingdom demands nothing less.

What have we just witnessed at our seminary? Has the dominant system in power won yet again? I hope not. Regardless of what their motives are, our leaders here have failed us, and they have failed the church. The board has failed us under the pretense of Gospel justice. The administration has failed us under the pretense of Gospel action. While all of the faculty are victims, most of the faculty are not here to teach us, to pray with us, and accompany us in ministry. At least not yet.

As future leaders of the church, what are we to take away from the events of the last month? Many people have said during the midst of this crisis that their decision to attend our seminary has been strengthened, not shattered. I said that myself a couple of weeks ago. I still believe that I am called here if only for this very moment.

In this morning's Gospel, Luke tells us that Jesus turns his face to go to Jerusalem. Jesus knows full well what waits for him there, but he turns nonetheless to make the difficult sacrifices faithful, authentic Gospel living requires.

We are called to make that turn ourselves, and especially today, the first day back after these historic actions. We each must make our own turn toward New Jerusalem. For some of us, that turn will lead us right back here. For others of us, that turn will take us to another seminary. Those who sent us here expect us to make the difficult sacrifices faithful, authentic Gospel living requires. Our Commissions on Ministry do. Our Bishops do. Above all, Jesus does.

What does faithful Gospel living look like in this moment in this place? We will each have to answer that question as the Spirit so leads us. Remember one thing though. We have been called here in this moment to *bear witness* to the events that took place here on Thursday and Friday. Never forget what we saw. Pledge always . . . to ourselves, to one another, to the church, and to our God . . . *never* to repeat this failure of leadership again. There *is* another way. There must be another way, and there is no turning back. "Let the dead bury their own dead; but as for you, go and proclaim the kingdom of God." God's kingdom demands nothing less.

Amen.

Devotions at a Faculty Meeting: First Thoughts on God's Action

J. Paul Rajashekar, PhD

Luther D. Reed Professor of Systematic Theology at the former Lutheran Theological Seminary, Philadelphia (Reflections at faculty meeting, February 2, 2016, three weeks after the announcement of the closure of the seminary scheduled for July 1, 2017)

When we all heard the announcement about the Board of Trustees' intent to dissolve this institution (The Lutheran Theological Seminary at Philadelphia), I wasn't expecting the kind of news that we all heard. My immediate reaction was mixed. First, I was a bit shocked, and then I felt excited, and later I became somewhat apprehensive or skeptical. Let me share with you my reflections on these emotions.

First, I was shocked, I mean not entirely. I have known, I suppose we all have known, for some years that the fiscal situation of the seminary, like a significant number of other seminaries in the US, has not been stable. There were clear hints here and there about the precariousness of our institution's future. In a sense, we all were quite aware of the writing on the wall but didn't know how to read it or were perhaps afraid to read it. As faculty and administrative staff, we did faithfully what we were called to do or assigned to do. We seriously deliberated a great deal about the situation in theological education of the past few years, trying to imagine a "Flexible, Affordable and Relevant (FAR)" curriculum in order to accommodate the social and cultural changes in our society, and the recession of resources, including faith, experienced by our churches. We have tried to reevaluate our strategies and responses in regard to the appropriate mode of delivering theological education. The cost of theological education has become prohibitive to sustain free-standing theological institutions as financial support from our supporting constituencies has considerably declined. This is a fact we all know and understand fully: that a re-visioning of theological education on a sustainable basis is necessary.

From this perspective the board's unilateral action is understandable, though I was a bit shocked at first. I was shocked because the board and the administration lacked the courage and trust to openly engage in a conversation with the faculty and staff to lay out the options before making their decision. It also represented a total contempt or disdain toward the faculty and staff, many of whom have spent most of their careers serving the institution. By wiping the slate clean through dissolving the whole institution, they were getting out of any responsibilities toward the faculty and staff. I was shocked because all our theological commitments had no meaning in the governance of a theological seminary!

Second, later that evening, as the initial shock wore off, I felt somewhat excited. Surely, I thought to myself, here is an opportunity to rethink theological education. In my own mind, I tried to imagine how this could be done; what are the implications for our understanding of the church's mission and ministry in a seemingly post-Christian world? Later that evening, I read Facebook posts by the administration and a board member interpreting the announcement with reference to Isa 43:19: "God is doing a new thing . . . do you not perceive it?" It really baffled me! How does one perceive that a momentous decision by a small group of people can come to be understood in relation to God's plan? How can one claim that a corporate decision being marketed to the constituency is somehow "God doing a new thing"? How can one be sure of it? Is the proposed "new thing" God is supposedly doing really a good thing or was this a marketing ploy? I kept musing whether this is really about God doing a new thing or if it is a biblical legitimation for a corporate action. Isn't it too quick to claim that "God is doing a new thing" when what is announced is only an intent or a proposal to dissolve two historic institutions (Philadelphia and Gettysburg seminaries) and rebirth them in a new incarnation? With so many unanswered questions it seemed to me problematic to claim God's support for a human plan.

Please bear with me that these were my private thoughts that evening. I realized that we theologians and preachers (not to mention clever seminary administrators) are good at citing Scripture or providing theological justification for human plans. We all do it. We invoke the name of God to justify human decisions, usually done by those in authority who confidently claim to know the mind of God. This is an age-old strategy used by many throughout human history. Maybe God is doing a new thing, but as a human I don't quite perceive it, as some have asserted. I can't help but raise the epistemological question, "How do you know?" Only history will tell! Don't get me wrong, I do believe that God often does new things without our consent or collaboration. As humans we are always under the judgment and mercy of God and we are not really in control of our lives or our future or those of our institutions. And yet, it seems to me a bit presumptuous to claim a corporate decision as tantamount to God's intent. In my view, at best, it is pious preaching to fool people and, at worst, a form of theological manipulation.

The more I thought about the narrative about God doing a new thing I recalled to mind that in the Old Testament God doesn't obliterate the past to create something new. The past is real, the history of God's people is real, even when God wants to change course. God's covenants with God's people are real and are by no means revoked. God chooses to wipe out the transgressions of God's people, their unfaithfulness, from time to time, but God doesn't abrogate God's covenant to God's people, even when God does new things. God does new things to express God's compassion, to fulfill God's promises in response to the cries of God's people but not with the intent to destroy them. Israel is therefore called to remember the past as they walk into the future. The past is not behind them but before them. God doesn't rewrite the history of God's people as a clean slate, as if God has been absent in their history, nor is God unconcerned about their future. Only in light of the past is there a future.

This brings me to my third emotion: skepticism. The claim that God is doing a new thing among us is challenged by the writer of the Book of Ecclesiastes with a counter narrative in Ecc 1:1–11, especially vv. 9–11 ("What has been is what will be, and what has been done is what will be done; there is nothing new under the sun. Is there a thing of which it is said, 'See this is new'? It has already been done, in the ages before us").

I am not quite sure how to interpret these two verses. I leave it to you to exegete this passage for yourselves. It sort of resonated with me in light of what is happening in theological education. Having been involved in it for a long time, twelve years as the dean of this school, I know that theological education has always tried to reinvent itself but has yet to succeed in the Western world. No one for sure knows how theological education will evolve in the future. "The more theological education attempts to change the more it remains the same," the oft-repeated quote of Daniel Aleshire of ATS. Yogi Berra may have put it well: "It's déjà vu all over again!" Luther once said, "Change is easy, but improvement is difficult." What we think is new may very well turn out to be an optical illusion. All "new" curriculum, in my experience, has turned out to be a rehash of the "old!"

In the words of the author of Eccl 1:4, "A generation goes, and a generation comes, but the earth remains forever." There is transience about human existence on earth that really fails to bring us in touch with something that is absolutely new. If, therefore, we root our hope in the next generation or time, we are setting ourselves up for disappointment. It will simply not be that different. Nothing ever really changes except for the faces, the names, the methods, and perhaps the social/political dynamics. In fact, history repeats itself and no great thing emerges from "under the sun" that changes the essence of our existence here. We are born. We live and die. Others are born, etc. The world is a very repetitive place.

"There is nothing new under the sun. Is there a thing of which it is said, 'See this is new'? It has already been done, in the ages before us." It seems that the passage is so dismissive of the possibility of newness in our midst, contradicting our lived experience. We all know that the world changes, societies evolve, empires arise and fall, old Pharaohs pass away and new ones are installed, institutions die and are reborn, technological changes have really transformed human culture and civilizations over the course of history. These changes are real. Who can deny it? And yet, our skepticism persists. It seems all our plans and aspirations for newness in our mission and vocation, either reinventing the church or theological education, needs a healthy dose of skepticism. It is a folly to put our trust in our well-thought-out plans, strategies, efforts, and hidden agendas, if God is not behind them. We all know that our plans are not necessarily God's plans, despite our claims.

Let me conclude then that a healthy dose of skepticism is not a message of doom and gloom. It points to a future where God is in control. All human actions, individual or corporate, are under the judgment of God. Yes, there is nothing new under the sun! Here, at ground level, everything is pretty much the same generation after generation. But, the fact is that there is a God who rules over the sun who is compassionate and merciful! Meaning can be found only in relation to God, thus making life here tolerable, fulfilling, even delightful, and making our existence possible, through Jesus Christ. Amen.

Devotions at a Faculty Meeting: A Lenten Experience of Trauma

STORM SWAIN, PHD

Associate Professor of Pastoral Care and Theology at the former Lutheran Theological Seminary, Philadelphia (Reflections at the faculty meeting, March 6, 2017, four months before the merger with Lutheran Theological Seminary at Gettysburg, creating the United Lutheran Seminary)

In those days Jesus came from Nazareth of Galilee and was baptized by John in the Jordan. And just as he was coming up out of the water, he saw the heavens torn apart and the Spirit descending like a dove on him. And a voice came from heaven, "You are my Son, the Beloved; with you I am well pleased." And the Spirit immediately drove him out into the wilderness. He was in the wilderness for forty days, tempted by Satan; and he was with the wild beasts; and the angels waited on him.

MARK 1:9–13

THIS TIME SPEAKS OF the Lenten Journey, wilderness, the walk toward Jerusalem. We walk also toward the last days of LTSP. We are in the "between." That space between the resurrection reality of a new institution and the Good Friday experience of loss.

We cannot jump over the "Good Friday" experience, or the "Holy Saturday" space that follows, to get to the Resurrection. Despite the fact that I often critique people's use of Kubler-Ross' model of anticipated grief for all grief, we are indeed anticipating the loss of LTSP as an institution in itself. We are living into the impending loss and are grieving.

I learned as a hospital chaplain that it is hard to say "hello" to something before you have said "goodbye," and the other way around. We see this in parents who often need to hold the body of their stillborn child, to see who s/he was before they can let the child go.

However, the complicating factor for us is that this grief started with trauma, which in many ways has continued.

Recall the January (2016) meeting (of the faculty with the seminary president and chair of the Board of Trustees) in which we were anticipating an announcement about a merger with Gettysburg Seminary. Instead we were told that the two seminaries would be closed and a new school would be created; all faculty and staff would be laid off and "no preference" would be given to current faculty in hiring for the new seminary. (Months later the faculty were told that this would not be a closure of LTSP and LTSG, but a "merger" of the two, to make a new seminary. The language used at the time of publication is that of "consolidation.")

This was a traumatic loss. This loss was not about the closure of the seminary, but the loss of a relationship of trust and common mission between the faculty and the administration, between the faculty and the board, between the faculty and the vocations to which they felt called.

Janoff-Bulman (*Shattered Assumptions: Towards a New Psychology of Trauma*, 1992) suggests that trauma shatters three basic assumptions about the world. His assumptions, or descriptions of an embedded worldview, focus not on the symptomatology of trauma, which often gets pathologized, but on the level of meaning-making (or shattering). Janoff-Bulman thought that people tend to believe the world is benevolent and the world is meaningful, and that the self is worthy (perhaps in a Lutheran context I should say "of import" or "important").

Here at LTSP, we could reframe this in terms of the assumptions that may have been held before January last year.

- The seminary is benevolent.
- The mission of the seminary is meaningful.

- The seminary faculty is of worth in fulfilling the mission of the seminary.

Healing includes reconciling old shattered assumptions with new modified assumptions, or, as Serene Jones puts it, "reordering the collective imagination."

However, added to these assumptions is a fourth that focuses on "betrayal trauma."

- People are trustworthy and worth relating to.

"When traumatic events are perpetrated by trusted individuals," such as a seminary president or board, "this core assumption is shattered." After January, it felt like all these assumptions had been shattered.

In my own research on trauma, I was interested to find such grounded theory, arising out of the interviews with the chaplains who worked at Ground Zero (the site of the terrorist attacks of 9/11 in New York), that speaks to the impact of this interpersonal "betrayal trauma." Although those chaplains faced many potentially traumatizing factors in dealing with somewhat horrific material in blessing bodies and body parts, in close proximity with first responders who were personally attached to the lost, and many worked over a significant period of time, it was *not* the experience of the chaplaincy itself that was often most traumatizing. Several chaplains spoke of the sense of betrayal they felt, by those persons or institutions they expected to support them during this chaplaincy but did not: those churches that said they could do ministry "on their day off," or indicated that their chaplaincy work was "their thing, and not a ministry of the church." Interestingly enough, some chaplains who were in secular employment were told by their employers, "We'll keep you on full pay. You go down there and work one day a week, and we'll consider this our contribution to the recovery effort."

When we add interpersonal betrayal to trauma, grieving becomes complicated.

William Worden outlines four tasks of grieving that are particularly helpful in thinking about complicated grief: to come to terms with the reality of the loss(es), including material, functional, role, relational, intrapsychic, systemic; to process the pain of grief; to adjust to a new environment in which that which is lost is missing; and to find an enduring connection with that which has gone in the midst of embarking on a new life.

These tasks show us that working through trauma and grief is a process that takes time, attention to reality, and is relational.

We cannot skip attending to our "Good Friday" trauma, and the "Holy Saturday" space we have been living in for the last fourteen months, but we need to continue to find, as we have all be doing, a way to hold and handle it, to find a sense of agency and life in the midst of these losses. But we also know that we won't, like any other grief, "get over it." It has provided both a "heavy" end to LTSP, and a "heavy" beginning for the new institution, United Lutheran Seminary.

Mary Oliver's 2007 poem "Heavy" captures this process when she writes:

> That time
> I thought I could not
> go any closer to grief
> without dying
>
> I went closer,
> and I did not die.
> Surely God
> had his hand in this . . .

Resurrection reality is attention to new life, where God and laughter break in, in unexpected places. However, even the resurrected body of Christ is a scarred body. It will do us no favors to pretend otherwise. Yet, our God continues to call us—some of us to new places, some of us to this place in a new way, and for some of us, to what we don't know yet.

We live in "the now and the not yet," where we will have to find a new sense of mission, a way of making this meaningful, a sense of purpose rather than just function, and a way to build relationships of trust that are grounded in a reality that acknowledges the betrayal.

Like any journey into the wilderness, there will be temptations to take the easy way. We will see what happens in the days ahead.

2

Staying and Witnessing

God At The Site of Trauma

A. J. M. Irving, PhD

Assistant Professor of Religion and Heritage, Faculty of Theology and
Religious Studies, Rijksuniversiteit (Homily delivered September 15, 2014)

RECENTLY, AFTER A BUSY week of travel, writing, and speaking,
I climbed aboard a high-speed train for a week's holiday that
I had long promised myself: a week in Berlin. I did not know
quite what to expect as I alighted in that gigantic steel and glass
station, but I think it is safe to say that I secretly hoped for an
inexpensive, interactive, Bohemian theme park; an urbane and
slightly naughty hologram of a city, whose images would pleas-
ingly alternate between Prussian imperialism, 1920s cabarets,
opera, leftist book shops, pierced punk-rockers, and latter-day
environmentalist fairies. Sometimes, you understand, after a year
in a seminary, and a summer bent over manuscripts, one simply
feels the need to get out a little!

What struck me most about my experience of that great city
was, however, not its winsome combination of sophistication and
innovation, nor the cheeky juxtaposition of shiny new edifices of
governmental bureaucracy right alongside the overt celebration of
civil disobedience. What struck me in a way that I hadn't really expected were the ineradicable traces of the trauma of that city's past.

The disorientation begins almost as soon as one leaves the train station: instead of the usual jumble of fast-food shops, tobacconists, cheap hotels, and porn shops that jostle for attention around most European train stations, one is confronted in Berlin by . . . nothing at all: a large open space. Off in the distance one can see the new Norman Foster dome on the old Reichstag building, but then one realizes that one can see it only because of the empty space in between: everything was, of course, destroyed in the war.

All week long I found it difficult to walk around the city without being constantly reminded of a cataclysm. The tower of the Memorial Church, built at the pinnacle of German imperialism, stands now like some jagged tooth of a long-disintegrated corpse. The stately row of neoclassical columns surrounding the world-famous museums, shattered, cracked, and pock-marked by shrapnel, is a silent siren announcing the maelstrom and destruction of aerial bombing to passersby. Bright vistas of freshly reconstructed avenues, gates, and monuments take on darker hues when images of the same spaces swathed in swastikas and filled with military marches bleed from one's memory into one's current experience of the space. And little lines of bricks inlaid in the pavement that cut across the roads, footpaths, and squares of Berlin are scars in stone indicating with indelible precision just where the city was severed, where it was forced to live in exile from itself during the Cold War.

Of course, one does not need to travel as far as Berlin to encounter a space marked by trauma. Just a few stops down on the E train in this city, you can peer into two exactly constructed black holes, whose sides are constantly bathed with water streams that both evoke and at once transfigure the images we cannot forget of the devastating collapse of the twin buildings that stood above them. Often memorials are more makeshift: flowers left among the wreckage in a Ukrainian field; soft toys, candles, and notes in the middle of a street in Ferguson, Missouri; a white cross on a treacherous bend in a country road. Sometimes, there is no physical sign of the past catastrophe at all: battlegrounds are turned into car parks, school walls are painted over, the pavement scrubbed, and flower pots are cheerfully arranged in the windows of a place of chronic abuse; only the historically informed and the peculiarly sensitive bear witness to what happened in these places.

Today's feast invites us to approach a site of trauma. Since at least the early fifth century, Christians have marked the feast of the dedication in the year 334 of a basilica on the site in Jerusalem where, pious tradition holds, the Savior of the world was tortured and executed by Roman authorities. According to Eusebius of Caesarea, the church historian, in about 325 the emperor Constantine ordered the excavation of the site, the labor-intensive removal of infill and rubble that had been dumped there after the Romans' destruction of the holy city, and the demolition of the temple of Aphrodite, which had apparently been built at Golgotha.

How this precise site was relocated, when, as Constantine himself put it in a letter to the local bishop Eusebius, "the evidence of his most sacred passion, long since hidden under the ground . . . remained unknown for such a long period of years" is not known. Eusebius has Constantine rather deliberately setting out to "make universally famous and revered the most blessed site of the Savior's resurrection" by removing all the "filthy rubbish" by which it had been "consigned to oblivion and ignorance." Rufinus of Aquileia, writing some seventy-five years later, suggests that it was Constantine's mother, Helena, who, less concerned with the site of the resurrection than with that of Christ's death, asked the locals "where the sacred body . . . had hung fastened to the gibbet." She was, he writes, admonished by their advice, and by heavenly signs before she rushed to the place, pulled away "everything profane and defiled" and dug down deep to find beneath the rubble the instrument of our Lord's torture and death.

What is it that could make us want to dig with her? What is it that this feast day, every celebration of the Eucharist, every sign traced over our faces, every baptismal anointing, every cross gleaming from our windows, carved into our screens, or hanging around our necks, what is it about this fearsome, gruesome sign that could possibly draw us and all humankind to it?

We dig through the rubble, we hold on to the cross because it is here, even here, that we find God. We are drawn, we dig down, we hold on, we venerate, because we have learned with the Philippians to sing an encomium of praise of an unexpected kind of Savior, a "God otherwise." In his letter to the Philippians, Paul is happy to cite this church's own distilled account of the deeds of this Savior. No mention of celestial signs or prodigies in this encomium, no description of worthy lineage or ancestry. Nothing about physical prowess, nor virtues; nothing concerning Jesus' miracles, teachings, or message; nothing even about the purpose or results of his death. At the heart of this brief passage is instead the account of one who, though in the form or mode of existence of God, was humiliated—humiliated in his obedience to the point of death. It was not suicide, not glorious heroism, but execution upon sentence by the same authorities, the same structures of power that the Philippians knew only too well. As the Lutheran biblical scholar John Reumann has written, the response to one such as this cannot be "Halleluiah, what a savior!" but "He is one with us," he is one with those who know precisely what it means to be humiliated by the world, its structures, hierarchies, violence, and economics. What is more, it is precisely this humiliated one, this one in the mode of existence of slave, whom God has superexalted. It is this executed Jesus, not Caligula nor Nero, whom the Philippians defiantly proclaim Lord.

As we utter the Philippians' confession of faith, as we celebrate the feast of the cross, we find ourselves strangely disoriented, in an unexpectedly large open space, as though a bomb has gone off, shattering all our simple notions of who God is and how God operates. What one theologian has called "our infantile desire's God of Marvels"—a God of power and the kind of justice that we can agree with, "a God all the more easily manipulable . . . [and] at the service of our ideologies since [his] sublime majesty is only the idealized projection of our own megalomania"—this notion of "God" has been burst open. In this Jesus, who was executed in the form of a humiliated slave, God himself is crossed out by the very people who would define what power and divinity and justice are. Eberhard Juengel puts it this way: it belongs to the being of God to come into the world only by "allowing God's self to be expelled from it," to come into the world as the humiliated one, crossed out by humankind.

This intolerable God, defying every established order (especially religious order) and every good reason (especially religious reasons) that human beings have given themselves about how God should operate—a God who is not for the good people and against the evil, a God who rewards those who show up late with the same wages received by the conscientious early birds, who throws a feast to celebrate the return of a squandering prodigal, who calls blind those who claim to see—cannot but be rejected, expelled, humiliated, and condemned to the kind of death reserved not for prophet martyrs, nor valiant heroes, but for rabble-rousers and criminals.

Confronted by this feast, kneeling in the pit with Helena and the construction-site workers, we find ourselves then not questioning the cross, but being questioned by it. What does the confession of a faith in a God like this, a God at the heart of trauma, imply about our relationships to each other "amid [all] the humiliations in Caesar's world?"

Do You Leave Your People to Die? Constance and Her Companions

Deirdre Good, ThD

Faculty, Stevenson School for Ministry, Diocese of Central Pennsylvania
(Sermon delivered September 8, 2014)

"THE PANIC IS FEARFUL today," wrote Constance, an Episcopal nun from Memphis, Tennessee, in the summer of 1878. "Eighty deaths reported and half the doctors refuse to report at all. We found one of our nurses lying on the floor in her patient's room down with the fever, another is sickening. I really believe that Dr. Harris and I and the two negro nurses are the only well persons anywhere near here."

As Jeanette Keith describes in her 2012 book *Fever Season: The Story of a Terrifying Epidemic and the People Who Saved a City*, ravages of yellow fever in the summer of 1878 in Memphis forged the city's identity for generations to come. It was a saga that capsized conventional nineteenth-century American views of heroism. All but one of the city's white Baptist ministers left the city. A prominent politician on a trip out of town deserted his family. African-Americans, who were rumored to be immune to the disease, stepped up as militiamen and police officers, providing essential security for the relief effort. And in one much-celebrated instance, a prosperous madam sent her girls away and converted her brothel to a hospital, where she nursed the sick until she was killed by the fever herself.

From August to October 1878, the people of Memphis suffered through an experience unique in American history. Yellow fever is a viral hemorrhagic fever passed from human to human by mosquitoes. Although mild cases produce flu-like symptoms, at its worst yellow fever is comparable to Ebola. The virus strain that caused the 1878 epidemic was extremely virulent. The fever spread up the Mississippi Valley from New Orleans to Illinois and killed an estimated eighteen thousand people. But it was Memphis's plight that riveted national attention. At least two thirds of the people in Memphis contracted the fever, and about one quarter died, more than five thousand in all.

This is a week for thinking about our response to death: from today's gospel of John 12 in which the gospel narrator and a voice from heaven witness to the death and expansive glorification of a grain of wheat; to the martyrdom of Constance and her companions whose lives we remember today; to the lives of those who are ill, dying, and who have died from the Ebola epidemic in Liberia, Sierra Leone, and other parts of West Africa, apparently now spiraling out of control; and on Thursday those who died on September 11, 2001, and who are still affected and dying from the aftermath of the destruction incurred while ministering to workers and others at Ground Zero, amongst them our own graduates. So, let's be clear: this is not a week in which we reflect from a triumphalist perspective on the successful eradication of yellow fever from Memphis and other parts, or any other victory in the wake of 9/11, or the diminishing flood of Ebola patients. In fact, the opposite is the case. We are here to reflect on what it was like to be present, to live and minister in Memphis in 1878; what it is like to live and minister in Nigeria, Guinea, Sierra Leone, and Liberia in the midst of the Ebola outbreak; what it was like to live through 9/11 in New York City and even here in our seminary community. We are here to ask about our response to a crisis: do you leave your people to die or do you stay, help, and bear witness?

Josephine Finda Sellu, deputy nurse matron in a government hospital in Sierra Leone, lost fifteen of her nurses to Ebola and thought about quitting herself. But in the end, she did not. "There is a need for me to be around," said Ms. Sellu, who oversees the Ebola nurses. "I am a senior. All the junior nurses look up to me." The *New York Times* of August 24 reports, "She resembles a Field Marshall in light brown medical scrubs, charging forward, exhorting nurses to return to duty, inspecting food for patients, doing a dance for once-infected coworkers who live, and barking orders from the head to toe suit that protects her from her patients. . . . There are times when she says, 'Oh my God, I should have chosen secretarial.' But her job as a healer, she said, 'is the calling of God.'"

"We had to face our own mortality that day as we fled Trinity Wall Street carrying children to the ferry. . . . I was glad to be carrying a child but I worried we'd not survive or that if we did, that they'd all be orphans as their parents worked in the World Trade Center," Father Lyndon Harris, rector of St. Paul's Chapel, said of 9/11. When he returned fearfully to the site the next day, he was astonished to find that St. Paul's was spared not, as he later reflected, because it was particularly good but because it had a big job to do and a mission to fulfill. On that first day, as he left St. Paul's, an exhausted firefighter on Broadway asked to sleep in the church, but Father Harris said "no." He was worried that the building would collapse. So instead, while waiting for the structural analysis of the church, he set up a food concession stand outside the church for the workers with the help of Seamen's Church Institute and other volunteers by handing out barbecue-grilled hamburgers on Broadway. Indeed, he said, "There was nothing we wouldn't do for the trauma of the workers at the 9/11 site for eight and a half months. We had thousands of volunteers."

He describes life at Ground Zero: "Walking through the site every day was very intense—I could hear every human emotion, see the melting boots and shoes and paws at the longest burning site in this country's history, but we discovered in the course of living through it that we could be more courageous, more generous, and better than we ever imagined." "On the day we closed," he said, "one of the construction workers asked to say something." These are Tom Gerrity's words: "I really didn't want to come to Ground Zero because my sister-in-law was killed and I cursed God. But as a construction worker, I couldn't escape it. Little by little I came to get food at St. Paul's and my heart opened back up. When I was hungry, you were a little café on Broadway; when I was distressed, you were a therapist's couch; when I needed inspiration, you were a concert hall and an art gallery" (thousands of children's letters were posted all over the place).

Reflecting on the whole experience, Father Lyndon Harris says that what happened at St. Paul's was nothing short of the kingdom of God. "We had corporate workers honored to be offering sandwiches to construction workers and we had different religious congregations volunteering every day." We had some people say, "When are you going to be a church again?" I said, "Come on! This is a church; this is what the kingdom of God is every day. Every day we have Eucharist."

Through such life-threatening situations as these we learn that we cannot protect people from pain and that there is often nothing that we can do for survivors and the traumatized other than to listen, to care, and to bear witness in the midst of all the pain and suffering. Many are injured and many will die, and all we can say is that we can create a record of all that happened so that your story will be told, and that we will be your witness.

Eye of the Storm

David Hurd, MusD, DSM, LHD

Organist and Music Director, The Church of St. Mary the Virgin, New York City
(Sermon delivered Tuesday in Holy Week, April 15, 2014)

Tonight is like being in the eye of a storm. We are in a relatively quiet moment in the midst of great surrounding turbulence. Most of us began last Sunday to suspend so-called real time and enter a week-long re-presentation of events quintessentially at the heart of who we are called to be. Through the testimony of St. Matthew, we witnessed and felt the exhilaration of a people's long-hoped-for salvation, identified and celebrated as Jesus was proclaimed King and entered Jerusalem with great Hosannas. But the story continued, and we witnessed and felt a spectrum of discomforts as the whole plan seemed rapidly to derail in a shocking trial and execution of the same hoped-for Savior. For us this cannot simply be a cliff-hanger to keep us in suspense pending "a happy issue being made out of all this affliction" (in the phraseology of the Book of Common Prayer), but rather it is a gift of *time* to reflect more deeply on the multiple layers of this story, which is *our* story. There are many ways of doing such reflection, including the reading of Scripture, commentaries, and the writings of wise and recognized theologians. Sitting in silent contemplation is a practice of some. Many will reflect through the lens of great musical works. Such masterpieces as the St. Matthew or St. John Passion of Bach, Handel's "Brockes" Passion or his "Messiah," are great gifts to humankind, and especially to those of faith. Other more recent works such as John Stainer's "Crucifixion," Leo Sowerby's "Forsaken of Man" or Krzysztof Penderecki's 1966 "St. Luke Passion" also juxtapose Scripture and devotional texts in their respective composer's distinctive musical vocabularies. Wordless musical works such as Marcel Dupré's "Stations of the

Cross" for organ also help focus reflection. However, I now ask you to come with me through this verbal meditation.

Paul writes to the Corinthians that the message of the cross is foolishness to some, but the power of God to those being saved. Here we are in what appears to be an ocean of contradictions. This is the time and this is the place where everything is upside down and nothing is as it seems it should be. This is the time and this is the place where weakness is power, and strength is weakness; where folly is wisdom, and wisdom is foolishness; where the despised is exalted, and the highly placed is degraded; where the living are perishing, and the dying are being saved; where things which are not are supplanting those which are; where an instrument of humiliation and torturous death becomes the defining sign of love and eternal life.

Isaiah's words describing divine thoughts not as human thoughts and divine ways not as human ways, are a refreshing reminder to us that we are part of God's creation, and not the other way around.

Our reading from Isa 49 tonight concerns Israel's restoration and mission. God's promise precedes and follows the set-backs and frustrations that seem to want to invalidate it along the way. As a church, we have spent five weeks of special devotion. Invited, as we were on Ash Wednesday, "to the observance of a holy Lent, by self-examination and repentance; by prayer, fasting, and self-denial; and by reading and meditating on God's holy Word," the words of Isaiah's song to search and call for the Lord with the assurance of God's compassion are all the more compelling. Our repentance, our turning to God, is rooted in God's promise of mercy. According to Isaiah, *God* is establishing the time frame: "while he *wills* to be found . . . *when* he draws near." Nevertheless, the Canticle closes with the assurance that God's promise *is* to be fulfilled, God's purpose *accomplished*—a restored creation.

On this Tuesday of Holy Week—and now in the eye of the storm—we have been to Jerusalem and, through Matthew's eyes, we have seen Jesus enter the city in peculiar splendor and leave it with Simon of Cyrene compelled to carry the cross on which Jesus would be *crucified*. Crucifixion was at the most horrid extreme of means for public execution. It was not only about eventual death; it was also about the cruel infliction of prolonged agony and public humiliation. In his day, Constantine abolished crucifixion as a legal punishment, although, according to the Oxford Dictionary of the Christian Church, "isolated instances were recorded later in the fourth century." Twelve centuries later, in 1597, six Franciscan friars and twenty of their converts were crucified at Nagasaki. That seems shockingly recent; we commemorate them on February 5 each year as the Martyrs of Japan. In our more civilized modern day we have hanging, decapitation by guillotine, firing squad, gas chamber, electric chair, lethal injection, and other "humane" forms of civilly imposed death, although certain hate crimes such as the killing of Matthew Shepard sixteen years ago in Laramie, Wyoming, might seem to derive their sadistic inspiration from the even more brutal practices of our Lord's day. Today, those who wish to cheer, jeer, and leer at executions are sometimes held at slightly more discrete distances than in our Lord's day, although traces of the vengeful mob can even be observed in our own time. What scandal and embarrassment and absurdity, this crucifixion in Jerusalem. Has human behavior changed much since then? For the message of the cross is foolishness to some, but the power of God to those being saved.

Who are *"those* who are perishing?" Who are *"us* who are being saved?" Here in this place we are teachers and students together; we seek wisdom, even the Way of Wisdom. Folly or foolishness are seen in contrast to, or as the opposite of, Wisdom by St. Paul in his letter to the Corinthians. Foolishness, to paraphrase Robert Sternberg, is the lack or failure of wisdom and of making proper careful choices. In this sense, it differs from *stupidity*, which is the lack of *intelligence*. Intelligence may actually be more easily measured and quantified than wisdom. Academic institutions like ours are typically set up for measuring intellectual grasp, and even fostering competition among its constituents. This can be healthy and creative as we encourage one another's growth in wisdom. But what goals are we prepared to measure, and how will we rate our success? Can we, individually or collectively, bring our faith to its perfection, as if we could then bottle it and market it, presumably to the church, like Perrier to the cocktail lounge circuit. Can *wisdom* or *ministry* any more be a *product* than the church itself can be a *business*, without suffering the corruptions of commerce and politics?

John writes in the portion of the Gospel we heard tonight that even though many authorities believed in Jesus, from fear of the Pharisees they would not acknowledge it, since they clung to human praise over praise of God. Pride, politics, personal advantage: when it comes to those who are perishing and us who are being saved, might some of *us* actually be *them*? The message of the cross is foolishness to some, but the power of God to those being saved. And Paul promises from Isaiah that God destroys the wisdom of the wise.

In contrast, the seventh chapter of Wisdom personifies her as more mobile and subtle than any movement; a wisp of God's breath, an emanation of God's glory, and an image of God's goodness. What we have here is not a wisdom limited to cleverness or intellectual virtuosity, which, left to its own devices, fails to do much more than congratulate itself on its own skillfulness. Rather, it is that to which we are continually drawn. It is wisdom in which the cross ceases to be a stumbling block, and becomes the means of turning right-side up those things that have been upside down, giving us a glimpse of God's higher thought. It is wisdom through which we may see and begin to know what has been done for us in Christ Jesus. It is wisdom that can bring us to join with Paul in declaring, as he wrote to the Philippians, that nothing surpasses knowledge of Christ Jesus for whose sake all can be lost in the face of gaining and being found by Christ.

So here we are, in the eye of the storm, in what appears to be an ocean of contradictions. This is the time and this is the place where everything is upside down and nothing is as it seems it should be. This is the time and this is the place where weakness is power, and strength is weakness; where folly is wisdom, and wisdom is foolishness; where the despised is exalted, and the highly placed is degraded; where the living are perishing, and the dying are being saved; where things which are not are supplanting those which are; where an instrument of humiliation and torturous death becomes the defining sign of love and eternal life. For the message of the cross is foolishness to some, but the power of God to those being saved.

3

Flight or Fight

God Is Not a Microwave

REVEREND HERSHEY MALLETTE STEPHENS

Associate Rector, St. John's Norwood, Chevy Chase, Bethesda, Maryland
(Sermon and commencement Eucharist delivered May 20, 2015)

Go therefore and make disciples of all nations baptizing
them in the name of the Father and of the Son and of the
Holy Spirit, teaching them to obey everything that I have
commanded you. And remember, I am with you always,
to the end of the age.

MATT 28:19–20

TODAY, I STAND BEFORE you with an incredible task. I am charged
with bringing you Good News when all I can think about is how I
am angry and sad.

Today, I am also reminded of something my beloved Professor Andrew Irving once said to me in the fall of my second year
in seminary. I remember coming to class, and much like I did today, I announced my vexation and misery. I was frustrated and
bewildered about any number of things that were happening in
2013: the school had no money, my classmates were transferring

or withdrawing, and on top of all that, there was a cookie shortage in the refectory! Professor Irving, in his wisdom said, "Hershey, Jesus did not promise you happiness."

With that, let us return to the text:

> Go therefore and make disciples of all nations baptizing them in the name of the Father and of the Son and of the Holy Spirit, teaching them to obey everything that I have commanded you. And remember, I am with you always, to the end of the age.

I've read this text countless times. Only recently, a little something stuck out. And when I say a little something, I mean a very little something.

It's that comma in the very last sentence of Matthew that literally gives me pause. The comma, or pause, used in this last sentence sets off what is formally called a parenthetical element, but most of us would just call it extra information. But in this case, this added information gives focus to the original idea.

I am with you always, to the end of the age.

I once had a conversation with Mother Mitties about this comma, and she pointed out that in Greek there is no punctuation. However, I don't read Greek, so I'll trust that the good Holy Ghost–filled people who translated the NRSV employed a comma in this sentence for a reason.

Either way, I'd like to offer you my own translation: The Hershey Mallette Community Colloquial Version of Matt 28:19–20:

> Jesus says, "Go out into the streets, hit the blocks, every ghetto, every city, every sleepy suburban place; live with the people as you work to bring God's Kingdom. Baptize them—bring them into the familial bond of the Father, Son, and Holy Spirit. Teach them about the liberation in God's love. And know, I got your back, 'cause this just might take a while."

I am with you always, to the end of the age.

If you leave here today, and remember nothing else that I have said, remember this: God Is Not a Microwave!

But hear this! Slow work does not mean you can say "no" to the work.

God is not a microwave. God seldom does anything instantaneously, rapidly, or straightaway. I'm sure you know this, especially after spending any amount of time at this seminary.

God didn't make the world in an instant.

God didn't flood the earth, or cause floodwaters to recede the day after Noah's boat beached.

God didn't make Abraham a nation in prompt fashion.

God is not a microwave.

God didn't deliver the people of Israel from Pharaoh instantaneously.

God didn't deliver Moses from the wilderness directly.

God didn't make Israel listen immediately—how many times did the prophets say that to the same people? And poor, poor Job: how long did the restoration of that one household take?

God is not a microwave.

God didn't restore Jerusalem overnight.

God didn't make the dry bones live in an instant . . . it took time!

First, they rattled. Then the bones came together. Then the tendons and the sinews attached themselves. Then the flesh appeared. And the skin covered that flesh. That's four or five reconstructive steps before those bones even had breath.

God is not in the business of rapidly and carelessly creating or restoring anything.

God didn't bring any of us seminarians through our respective discernment processes quickly.

Our staff, and our registrar, can testify that God has not inspired me to move speedily to submit any of my forms throughout this entire three years!

And God must be taking a sweet time fashioning every heart and mind in this room to know what it means to do justice, love kindness, and to walk humbly with God.

I could go on and on and on about how slow our God is, but I think you get my point. God takes God's time. So, knowing that we serve a God who will outwait us, and is in no rush to smooth over, cover up, and justify the pain of our past year, we cannot fall victim to the temptation of what theologian Dorothee Soelle calls Christian sadomasochism.

Christian sadomasochism looks at any situation where God's people are getting hurt, where God's people are suffering, and says that it's all for the best, because we'll grow from the pain. In our hurry to move on, we want to justify suffering so fast that we've almost already convinced ourselves that the events of this past year have actually made us a better seminary.

Some would like to convince us that the catastrophe that stunted the spiritual and material work of our community this year has been in our best interest. Yes, there are such things as growing pains. But there's also unnecessary suffering that God did not intend for us. There is avoidable, worthless, man-made suffering. We've had our share of that this year. We cannot claim to be disciples of Christ and twist man-made pain into God-ordained suffering on a redemptive cross.

Friends, we now must make up for lost time!

Can you imagine a time in history when the world needed those of us who call ourselves disciples more than in the past year? More than it does now? Social movements, resistance, and revolutions are erupting all across the nation and world. The people in the cities are crying out to God and to the church. And while cities and hearts were on fire, we have been stuck here wasting time trying to detangle ourselves from the webs of privilege and patriarchy that threaten to strangle the love of God.

James Baldwin writes, "Not everything that is faced can be changed, but nothing can be changed if it is not faced." If we try to write the history of the past year as something we went through together and have now emerged from on the other side as a stronger community and school, then we are doomed to repeat the same mistakes.

God is not a microwave.

I am not precluding personal growth out of adversity. Lord knows I wouldn't be standing here on the shoulders of my ancestors if I didn't believe in that. There are no limits to God's redemptive powers. But that fact doesn't let us off the hook.

To love this school, to love this church, to love ourselves, we have to tell the truth about ourselves. The only hope we have is in God, who promises to outwait us; in Jesus, who came to Earth in solidarity with the marginalized, to liberate us, to make the dream of God known. And in the lavish gifts of the Holy Spirit fortifying us to fight structures of power, principalities, and the spiritual forces of evil.

But God is not a microwave.

I think that is why Jesus says at the commissioning, I am with you always *comma* to the end of the age.

Yet God's slow work does not mean no work. The fact that God is slow does not absolve us from the mission Jesus has given us. In fact, it means that our work is all the more urgent! We have no time to waste. We must listen to Jesus.

Go! Make disciples! Baptize believers! Teach people to love God, and each other! And remember, I am with you always, to the end of the age.

This commissioning is hard work; it is challenging!

How do we make disciples? Making disciples is more about what we are doing than about indoctrinating, selling, or convincing others that we have a good thing that they need or should want.

We make disciples when we discipline ourselves to honor the particularities in the lives of all people to whom God has entrusted the care of community, and to hold their stories with reverence.

We make disciples when we welcome LGBTQI folks in our churches as family members and siblings, and firmly and in love challenge those among us who seek to put limits on a limitless God.

We make disciples when we work for the freedom of the oppressed. When we personally and as an institution attend to the ways that racism, sexism, and homophobia have crept into the fabric of our Episcopal Church lives, shrouding our communities and our best efforts like paraments.

I know we all think we are way too learned and sophisticated to ever be racist, sexist, or homophobic. But before you tune me out by listing in your brain all the black folk, women, queer folk, and poor folk in your churches, I beg you stay with me. If it were true, if we were too evolved to be racist, sexist, or homophobic, then we wouldn't need to proclaim good news to hearts broken by the misuse of power and irresponsible exercise of privilege in this room, in this church, and in this world.

This is not political work; this is spiritual work. If you leave today saying you heard a political sermon this morning, you've missed the point. This is a matter of the soul: yours, mine, all of ours here today. This is a sermon drawn from the Gospel promise of liberation and life. This is a sermon about Jesus!

The truth is, when we engage in the beautiful chaos of community, people will want to be with us. We will baptize them to welcome them to this family making its slow march through time and space toward the Kingdom of God. We baptize in the name of Love that created all things; in the name of the One who embodied Love, and in the name of the One who is the presence of Love in our everyday lives. The thing that is so important and so incredible about baptism is that it is an experience that bonds us forever in love to God, and we have absolutely no idea what that means!

Living into our baptism, into discipleship, is when the hard work of this mission continues. Teaching disciples is to obey all that Jesus commanded. Jesus commanded us to love God with all our hearts, souls, and minds, and to love our neighbors as ourselves. How do you teach this countercultural, non-instinctive, unpopular way of existence?

Other than living it, I have no clue. But here is what I have learned about love. I have learned that love is uncomfortable. And trying to make love comfortable is what makes it even more uncomfortable. It's like planning every outfit for dates with coordinating makeup and accessories. Or trying to be on your best behavior and practicing your lines to make sure that what said is exactly the right thing in every situation. The desire for perfection, the desire for perpetual prettiness, is what makes love unbearably uncomfortable. In fact, it is a lie and there is no love in that.

I learned that meeting the uneasiness of connecting is love. That involves always knowing you could be wrong. And doing lots of listening with the understanding that "wherever you stand, someone just as reasonable, rational, and good as you stands in an opposite place. You stand there by faith." Love means knowing when you have said enough; knowing when you need to take a break. Ultimately, loving requires great amounts of self-awareness and honesty. It's tedious, and it's tense, but it's true.

I think teaching people about God's love is all about the way we understand love in our closest relationships. Perhaps one way we embrace and teach Jesus' command to love God and our neighbor is through the super-slow work of creating trusting relationships in community and in the church. This totally axes the top-down shallow model of corporate church growth, where politics and proclivities are taboos. The love Jesus commands his disciples to live is a love that values mutuality, relationships, and shared experiences.

This love requires us to be in continual prayer, to be delivered from the love of comfort, from pursuit of fortune and fame, from the fear of serving others, and from the fear of death or adversity. I believe that is why at the end of the commissioning in Matthew Jesus says, "And remember, I am with you always, to the end of the age."

This is hard, messy, slow work!

"I am with you always, to the end of the age" is the assurance that our marvelously meticulous God is working through each and every one of us. With great care, and painstaking strategy, the God of providence is fulfilling the ultimate meaning of existence, within every eon, every era, and age.

The Good News is this—God has made provision for each of us, in the person of Jesus Christ. We approach this altar perhaps for the last time together, to present ourselves, our souls, and our bodies, to be made one body with Jesus in prayer, so our habit becomes righteousness and our instinct kindness. So that with Jesus at the head, our work may continue to bring in the Kingdom.

We disciples make our sacrifice of thanksgiving not just this graduation day, but every day. So, let the Spirit in you baptize all that you encounter in every ghetto, every city, and every sleepy suburban place. Proclaim the freedom of our God in Jesus to every language, people, and nation. And model the saving possibilities of following Jesus' commandment to love in every situation.

That is our mission! And it isn't for the faint of heart, or for the compulsively tidy. And frankly, some days you just won't be feeling it!

We go back to the text for help. The commissioning begins, "When [the disciples] saw [Jesus], they worshiped him, even though some doubted." The disciples worshiped Jesus, even though some doubted. Our call is to do the same, knowing that all authority in heaven and on earth has been given to Jesus!

We worship Jesus, even though we doubt.

We worship Jesus, even though our school is in turmoil.

We worship Jesus, even though it seems no one will come to our rescue.

We worship Jesus, even though our friends, mentors, and colleagues are moving on.

We worship Jesus, even though you may not have a first call or a job.

We worship Jesus, even though our debt-to-income ratio is nuts!

We worship Jesus, even though black women and black men are being slain in the streets by state violence.

We worship Jesus, even though women make 80 percent of what men make, *even* in our church.

We worship Jesus, even though there are those among us in the church who wish for the return of the "glory days of the 1950s."

We worship Jesus, even though justice seems far off!

We worship Jesus, even though our mission is hard, painful, and grueling.

We worship Jesus, even though we may be sad and angry.

We worship Jesus, even though we have seen the worst and the ugliness of church institutions.

We worship Jesus even though we doubt, and we make disciples, baptize, and we teach love.

We worship Jesus, as we participate in the slow, attentive, and compounding work of Love. This is our mission!

And this mission should give us pause . . . only because stopping is not an option.

4

Marginalization

Be Strong, Do Not Fear. Here Is Your God

THE REVEREND ANDREW KADEL

Interim Rector, Calvary Episcopal Church, Flemington, New Jersey (Sermon delivered September 6, 2015, at Trinity Episcopal Church of Morrisania, Bronx)

Happy are they who have the God of Jacob for their help! Whose hope is in the Lord their God; who made heaven and earth, the seas; and all that is in them; who keeps his promises forever; who gives justice to those who are oppressed, and food to those who hunger.

ON JUNE 17, NINE members of Mother Emanuel AME Church in Charleston, South Carolina, were shot and killed by an attacker expressing reasons for the murders connected with race. The African Methodist Episcopal denomination has asked all churches in this country to join in a "Confession, Repentance, and Commitment to End Racism Sunday." The leadership of the national Episcopal Church and Bishop Dietsche have encouraged all parishes to participate, so I will focus on this issue in today's sermon.

Most Episcopal churches have a predominantly white membership. I have spent most of my ministry in parishes, which, though they often sincerely expressed a desire to be more diverse and inclusive, were slightly whiter in membership than the surrounding community. So being at this church has been a new experience for me and I hope I have learned something that may be relevant.

Racism . . . is actually difficult to recognize when you are its beneficiary. I'm serious, and I only really came to appreciate that fact as I experienced seeing the same human dynamic in other people in an entirely unrelated area over the past year. As I grew up, everyone expected me to do well in school and to be successful in a career. I learned that we all had rights and, that in a free country, we could exercise those rights without fear. I became used to being respected and trusted, given the opportunity to speak my mind and given the benefit of the doubt if I didn't get things quite right. I was aware that was not the experience of everyone, in particular persons of color, but it was a little hard to grasp why or how this came to be. About a year ago, a group of us quietly spoke the truth about some serious concerns, fully expecting to be taken seriously and brought into a conversation to solve the problems. I won't go into the specifics, but I suddenly experienced not being trusted, having my motives and interpretations of facts dismissed, and being cast out from all influence and receiving no respect. This was happening at the same time that our country's attention was focused on the much more important, literally life-and-death events in Ferguson, Missouri. I realized that what I experienced in being not respected or trusted, in a really limited and temporary way, was analogous to the lifelong experience of millions in our country: chronically not trusted, nor given respect as a matter of course, experiencing one sort of demeaning treatment or other and having the benefit of the doubt given to those who demeaned them. The difference was that I was dealing with a contained set of people and interests, but for millions, indeed for our country as a whole, these problems are defined by race.

It is easy enough to see violence, and bad words, and over-the-top racist nastiness. For Episcopalians, that generally happens far away and outside of our social group. We can safely be outraged, condemn bad language and bad actions, even pass resolutions or send money, then pat ourselves on the back, go back to business as usual, and everything stays the same. But what is difficult is to really see racism. One author helpfully labels it, PWS—Polite White Supremacy. Episcopalians are far too polite for Crass White Supremacy, but when you think of the Polite version . . .

Oh, no. We are far too good and Christian for that. . . . It would be rude to imply that any of our brothers and sisters in Christ ever profited from slavery. Oh, well maybe historically, but . . . still we need to be courteous and polite.

To be fair, most people's lives are a struggle. Comparing miseries doesn't help, most people experience their own difficulty and that is bad enough. They have a hard time imagining how they would get by and be able to properly take care of their children, or get to the point that they could have children, if anything of significance was taken away from them. And most people try to be good and try to find a way to see themselves and their families and friends as fundamentally good; that's how people survive.

The problem, put simply, is that the legacy of chattel slavery is indigestible for white Americans. I'm convinced that the concept of race as we have inherited it really developed from the need to rationalize and make morally okay the practice of keeping people of African ancestry in permanent bondage. That had evolved into a perception of economic necessity, so the rationale became that these people were enslaved because their race made it appropriate or even necessary for them to be slaves. Slavery itself was legally abolished more than 150 years ago, but its legacy in racism continues.

It is difficult to see how an ordinary guy whose family never owned a plantation or who doesn't have a family fortune going back to the slave trade profits from racism. Believe me, it's hard for that guy. But the benefit of unacknowledged privilege, of easier access to pathways to success, to safety and education that can be taken for granted—that is real. The problem is, even with those benefits things are not always easy and when you think about change. . . . Change is good, change the bad things, but the problem is, well . . . change. Change knocks our security free from its anchor; it might endanger things that are important to us, we might lose what we don't want to give up, and if you press this too far, the story of how we are good people might need to be changed.

So, the problem with race and the Episcopal Church is that on the one hand we can't afford to treat one category of people differently than another. As our lesson from James this morning says, "My brothers and sisters, do you with your acts of favoritism really believe in our glorious Lord, Jesus Christ?" Yet it will require much change, not just in a few rules but in our relationships and expectations of one another, changes that have implications for the finances of the church and where the administrative energy of the church might go. And yet, I don't know if you have been around to many of the churches in the Diocese of New York, but most of them are hurting financially, and even the wealthiest churches are not as well off as they once were, with fewer parishioners and smaller budgets. There isn't a no-cost solution to racism, even the energy to pay attention to how we treat one another is hard to come by.

What I want is for those of us who are privileged to listen to what people who suffer from racism have to say. It will be only through careful listening and working hard to change our attitudes and our behavior that we ever have a hope of ending the evil that is racism. It's a long process; perhaps our grandchildren will be able to explain to their grandchildren how hard the process was. And, let us pray that those babies will have a hard time understanding that.

Racism is a process of denial. Denial makes everything slippery, everything is hard to change—you just get yes'd to death and nothing changes. The Episcopal Church extends denial beyond questions of race into most corners of its life. Perhaps if we can be forthright in speaking with one another on issues related to race, we can also be forthright about priorities about mission, about providing ministry for our churches, about the responsibility of laity and about how the ministry of all baptized people can be effective in this world. The Gospel challenges us all to change, to be more welcoming, to live in the overwhelming grace of God and to not keep it to ourselves. The Gospel challenges Trinity Church to change as much as any other, and that can be frightening—yet no more frightening than the alternative—to become rigid and blind and cease to be.

We are called by God to be God's people. Listen to these words from our lesson from Isaiah:

Say to those who are of a fearful heart, "Be strong, do not fear! Here is your God. He will come with vengeance, with terrible recompense. He will come and save you." Then the eyes of the blind shall be opened, and the ears of the deaf unstopped; then the lame shall leap like a deer, and the tongue of the speechless sing for joy. For waters shall break forth in the wilderness, and streams in the desert, the burning sand shall become a pool, and the thirsty ground springs of water.

Be strong, do not fear. Here is your God.

5

Power In Community

September 11, 2014

JOSHUA DAVIS, PHD

Dean of the Alabama Integrative Ministry School of the Episcopal Diocese of Alabama (Sermon delivered September 11, 2014)

ONE OF THE MOST striking things Danielle and I noticed when we moved to New York City last year was that everyone has a story about what happened on this day, thirteen years ago. It wasn't just that everyone had a story but that they were all so specifically linked to New York itself. Professor Owens told us that the planes hit just as he began his new position teaching here, and right as his son started a new high school across town. Imagine how terrifying that must have been! Sloan Hoffer told me how he and hundreds of people like him, who worked in the financial district, had to walk home to a different borough that day because the trains had been shut down. Even though they'd lived in the city all their lives, they didn't know how to walk home because they'd always traveled underground. Story upon story was told of concerned, safe parents, spouses, siblings desperately calling from other boroughs for people near the towers, unable to get through, and then that moment of extraordinary relief when they heard a voice on the other end, "Oh, thank you God! You're all right!"

To those of us, like Danielle and me who were elsewhere in the country, these stories were so significant because New York was ground zero. Even as we found ourselves wanting to talk about our experiences that morning in Nashville and Hartford, we had this sneaking feeling that our stories weren't quite the same as the locals, that in telling them we might be imposing on something that was a bit too private or intimate—a special trauma that we have no right to claim as ours too. The truth of the matter is, though, that the shock and terror of those events was all of ours. It belonged to everyone. We were not here to live through what many of you did, but we were all of us brought together, united with one another, and with you, when it happened. The late writer David Foster Wallace wrote a very important piece for *Rolling Stone*, chronicling his experience of the first three days of the event. The essay is entitled "9/11: The View from the Midwest," and it was published in the October 25, 2001, issue, only a little over a month afterward. The attacks go entirely unmentioned throughout the piece, except when he occasionally makes cryptic reference to what he calls "the Horror." The essay opens with concise epigraphic statements characteristic of Wallace's style: "Location: Bloomington, IL; Dates: September 11–13, 2001; Subject: Obvious; Caveat: Written very fast and in what probably qualifies as shock." I encourage you to track down and read the entire piece because of what it has to say about human community and the unusual unity that we Americans experienced after the attacks. In one particularly striking passage Wallace writes that by early Wednesday morning (the attacks were on a Tuesday), "Everybody has flags out. Homes, businesses. It's odd: You never see anybody putting out a flag, but by Wednesday morning there they all are." He continues:

> The point being that on Wednesday here there's a weird accretive pressure to have a flag out . . . [but] what if you just don't happen to have a flag? Where has everyone gotten these flags, especially the little ones you can put on your mailbox? Are they all from July 4th and people just save them, like Christmas ornaments? How do they know to do this? Even a sort of half-collapsed house

down the street that everybody thought was unoccupied has a flag in the ground by the driveway.

These flags, emerging as if from nowhere, were signs of unity. They were signs that these plain-spoken Midwesterners stood in solidarity with those "sophisticated" East-coasters whom only yesterday they thought it their duty to mock and dislike. The flags were signs of the unity these Midwesterners had with one another. And woe unto you, if by Wednesday afternoon, you have no flag displayed on house or car, for ye shall be anathema to your people! The flags were signs of unity because the flag itself is understood to symbolize the strength and struggle to which we can all lay claim in this country—that struggle is for us, as the myth of Romulus and Remus was for Rome, the myth of our commonality.

But there is still something strange and unsettling about this unity. Where was it Monday morning? Where was it January–August of 2001? These Bloomington llinoians had expended a lot of energy before that Tuesday telling themselves and the world that they were everything those noisy, pushy New Yorkers weren't. They were salt-of-the-earth, corn-fed, blue-blooded America. And then on this day, thirteen years ago, suddenly: we are all the same?

Is the same true today? Hardly.

Please don't misunderstand what I am saying here. I am not making the moralizing point that the unity we had in the face of that tragedy is what we should have had before the tragedy. We heard a lot about that in the wake of the events when TV pundits and news commentators, like John Stewart, tried to shame us out of our partisan commitments. I suppose those are good observations to make, but what I'm proposing is different. I'm wanting us to think seriously about the unsettling fact that violence and destruction galvanized us on September 11, and in a way that unity with one another was something we were quite content to neglect on September 10 and before. Oh, perhaps we had known unity like this before. Maybe immediately after the attacks on Pearl Harbor or the assassination of John F. Kennedy. I was not born yet, so I cannot say. But that really is my point. Whatever unity we had with one another in the wake of these acts of violence certainly wasn't there for me to experience thirty or forty years later. That is, not without my own experience of national violence. And there's the truly disconcerting part: not that those of us around the country might not have had a right to claim New York City's trauma as our own, but that we only seem capable of imagining the reality of this unity, this shared, common life as some kind of stopgap, a reactive response to crisis, threat, destruction, coercion, retaliation, hatred, and violence.

And this is exactly what Jesus is talking about in today's Gospel reading. We can easily miss this because we are good twenty-first century mainline Protestants who've been trained to make the Gospel about universal morals. So our ears perk up when Jesus says, "Love your enemies," because we think this is a universal principle we can apply to any and every situation, an idea that means something that's supposed to be earth-changing but is really just a platitude, like, "All you need is love." But there is something else much more significant and demanding going on here. This passage is taken from that distillation of Jesus' teaching that in Luke is known as the Sermon on the Plain. Luke tells us that just before delivering this teaching, Jesus had spent the entire night on a mountain in prayer, and when he came down he designated twelve of his disciples as "apostles," who were to be the representative figures of the renewed twelve tribes of Israel. And in this teaching, Jesus is assuming an authority greater than Moses, both renewing and intensifying the communal obligations of Israel as set out in Exod 21–23 and Lev 19 and 25. Jesus is teaching the people how to live with one another in order to be the kind of community that exhibits the character of the God who called them out of slavery in Egypt.

In that time, under Roman Imperial rule, the common people of Israel suffered, and their communities began to disintegrate. So saying to them, "Love your enemies," was not a universal platitude—not some kind of social nicety that even the worst of tyrants would accede to. It was a radical, challenging task of creating a union where hostility, suspicion, and conflict had caused their common life to break apart. The high taxes imposed by

Roman hatchet men, in which some Israelites bought the right to collect from their fellow villagers, made life and its flourishing impossible for many. Families with stable sources of income and food were obligated by Torah to lend to those in need and to do so without expecting interest.

But the tax burdens were so heavy, even on them, that lending families often had to demand early repayment, and when the borrowers inevitably could not repay, communities were sent into a tailspin of economic insecurity. Hostilities were unleashed, and the ground was prepared for Jews to begin that practice that Israel's prophets had spoken of as the epitome of idolatry and infidelity: loaning money at interest.

To these people, Jesus says:

> I know you are exploited and I know it's unbearable. But rest assured: the rich and satisfied who laugh now have built their houses on sand, and when the flood comes they will be washed away. But if you do as I command, you who are poor, hungry, and weeping now, you will be happy, you will stand firm in the flood. So whatever you do, no matter how hard they press upon and provoke you, do not become like them. You must always continue to love one another, and loving one another means forgiving debts, just as Moses taught you. No matter how hard it gets, continue to share generously even with those whom you know cannot repay. Give to any who ask and don't ask for it back. And not only that, but when you've borrowed from someone you cannot repay and you are sued for your cloak, just strip naked and give your creditors all you have. Embarrass them, show them how stupid and self-destructive their behavior is. How they destroy not only your life, but their life too because they destroy our common life. Know this: Life can only thrive where there is mutual sharing, where there is true collaboration.

Moses had commanded a negative justice of equal retribution—"an eye for an eye." Jesus commanded a positive justice that gets out in front of transgression, one that forgives debts before it's even asked for, that seeks to bless before the curse is even spoken, that prays for the tyrant before he has executed his abuse. Note that Jesus does not command us not to have enemies or pretend that our enemies are really just our friends. No, he commands us to love them precisely because they are our enemies. That's a task infinitely more difficult than pretending you don't have enemies can ever be. Loving your enemies means you must be crystal clear about who they are because you have an obligation to the world to resist them. You have an obligation to refuse to make any common cause with those who are bent on destroying the good of us all.

We have tended to miss the fact that Jesus' teaching about turning the other cheek is not at all about deferential submission. In fact, Jesus is commanding defiance—defiance against all indignity and dehumanization. To this day, the left hand is taboo for people in the Middle East and in most of the world because it is reserved for personal hygiene. And during Jesus' day, striking someone with an open hand or a closed fist meant that your opponent was your equal. So the only way to strike a right cheek from the right side was to do so with back of your hand, in other words demeaning the other person by putting them beneath you. So turning the other cheek hardly means deference. It is a provocative act of defiant resistance. It is an active claim to dignity in the face of dehumanization, one that puts the aggressor in the impossible position of either doubling down on his intent to disempower you, thereby bringing shame on himself, or accepting you as an equal. Either way, the tables have been completely turned. This is important because it means that Jesus is not pronouncing a moral platitude, nor is he giving us a strategy for achieving a particular outcome. He is summoning a people whose very existence in the world is an exhibition of the true character and nature of God's power. That power has not even a hint of reactivity or defensiveness, for what has it to protect? That power is not roused by crisis, coercion, retaliation, or threats of violence and destruction. It recognizes these for what they are: the weak and self-destructive energies of death and evil, which are simply perversions of the vital powers of life that belong to God alone, the God who is merciful, forgiving enough to share Her power even with us. Mark it well: Jesus summons this people and commands them to live out this positive power of life in the world. This means not simply forgiving persons near us for offending our social sensibilities, but literally loving them, writing off the money they owe us, and generously, mercifully helping them when they are again in need. In other words, Jesus is summoning a people who live their life together in common according to a purely positive, creative, utterly active unity—a unity that is provocatively, radically defiant of all that tears us apart.

This is true power, although it looks to the world like vulnerability. It is that foolish power of the cross—an act of vulnerability and love so complete and positive that only it can actually be the form in which we encounter God's own power to create. It is a power strong enough not just to fell the powers and principalities of this world who rule it as enemies of God, but strong enough to knit us together in a unity with no hint of reactivity, to make us into a loving, forgiving people who are capable of confounding the machinations of evil and to remain standing even among the ruins of their thrones. Such is the vulnerability of Jesus. Such is the unity of the church. Such is the power of the love of God, which She has been generous enough to share with us.

The Ordination of Li Tim-Oi, First Woman Priest in the Anglican Communion, 1944

THE REVEREND DR. AMY BENTLEY LAMBORN

Visiting Professor of Pastoral and Contextual Theology, School of Theology,
University of the South (Sermon, January 24, transferred to February 26, 2015)

TODAY WE COMMEMORATE LI Tim-Oi as the first woman ordained priest in the Anglican Communion.

Li Tim-Oi was ordained a priest on January 24, 1944 in the Diocese of Hong Kong by Bishop Ronald Hall. And the Episcopal Church has officially designated January 24 for her commemoration. Today, February 26, is the anniversary of Li Tim Oi's death in 1992. In 2005, the graduating class gave as its gift to the seminary this icon of Li Tim-Oi, which usually hangs just behind this pulpit.

I have looked at our icon of Li Tim-Oi many, many times, usually as I have made my way to receive communion. By saying this, that I have *looked at* this icon, I am making a statement not so much about what I have done, as what I have *not* done. I have not gazed upon this icon in the manner of prayer. I have never *looked through it* in such a way that I might glimpse something of myself transformed, or in such a way that I might participate in the Holy Spirit's renewal of the world in a manner that is consonant with Li Tim-Oi's life and witness.

But after learning something about the rather complex truth of Li Tim-Oi's story, I think I am much more prepared to participate in such a transformative gaze. If you are like me and have only looked at this icon, perhaps you will be more prepared to gaze prayerfully on it, too.

Here is a bit of the official story of Li Tim-Oi, much as we might find it in *Holy Women, Holy Men*.

Named by her father "much beloved daughter," Li Tim-Oi was born in Hong Kong in 1907. When she was baptized as a student, she chose the name Florence in honor of Florence Nightingale, whom she greatly admired. After sensing a call to ministry in the church, Florence studied theology at Union Theological College in Canton. Upon her graduation, she first served the church as a lay leader and pastor, and in 1941 she was ordained a deaconess.

When Hong Kong fell to Japanese invaders some months later, and priests could not travel to celebrate the Eucharist, Bishop Hall, who had learned of Florence's ministry—including her ability to travel back and forth through occupied territory—decided to ordain her a priest. After World War II ended, Florence Li Tim-Oi's ordination suddenly became highly controversial. Bishop Hall was sharply criticized for not waiting on the church to come to unity about women's ordination. So, Florence made the personal decision to surrender her license as a priest until the larger Anglican Communion was willing to acknowledge her ordination.

Li Tim-Oi continued to find ways to serve the church without engaging in priestly ministry. But all that came to an end during the Cultural Revolution in China, when all the churches were closed. Li Tim-Oi was forced to work on a labor farm and, later, in a factory. She was suspected of engaging in counter-revolutionary activity, so she was required to undergo "political re-education."

In 1974 she was finally allowed to retire from factory work. Eventually, she was permitted to emigrate to Canada where several of her family members lived. To her great joy, she was licensed as a priest in the Diocese of Montreal, and later in the Diocese of Toronto, where she lived until her death in 1992.

There is a problem with this more or less "official" story of Li Tim-Oi. You see, this story leaves out some of the more challenging details and facts of her life—details and facts that give us a more honest and complicated picture.

For example, Li Tim-Oi did not so willingly surrender her priestly license by way of some sort of personal decision. She was *forced* to give it up due to the coercive pressure exerted by the church's leadership. During her forced labor on the farm and in the factory, Li Tim-Oi became so depressed and demoralized that she contemplated suicide. As an exercise of her political re-education, which is, of course, a euphemism for brainwashing, she was given a pair of scissors and forced to cut her priestly vestments to shreds. Li Tim-Oi was repeatedly shamed and humiliated by such psychological torture. And she was prevented from living out her vocation as a priest for more than thirty years.

The Rev. Mark Harris, a priest and blogger/commentator who has clearly looked *through*—not just *at*—Li Tim-Oi's life writes, "We must remember her as a woman whose vocation and ministry were severely curtailed and dismissed by the (Anglican) Communion, held in scorn by her government and unrecognized as a priest until the first flood of ordinations of women to the priesthood." Considering Li Tim-Oi's story in the larger history of the ordination of women, Harris adds, "The real lesson derived from the story of the ordination of women is that when unity and fellowship become the first priority of the church the result is end-less postponement of decision-making and the inequitable treat-ment of those most closely involved in the issue."

Looking even more broadly, and considering so many of our issues involving the lack of justice and integrity, I think we can say it this way: The church, in its various structures and bodies, has *repeatedly* engaged in this kind of endless postponement of decision-making, more often than not as a way of preserving the status quo, of giving the appearance or felt sense of hanging to-gether, or carefully guarding the privilege of a few. Meanwhile the people most closely and intimately involved are made to suffer—and sometimes to suffer mightily.

Earlier, we prayed for the Spirit to inspire us to follow Li Tim-Oi's example—"serving (God's) people with patience and happiness all our days, and witnessing in every circumstance to our Savior Jesus Christ." It is a lovely Collect, like so many of our Collects and prayers. But it seems to me that it is a prayer that is more associated with *looking at* Li Tim-Oi's life from a bit of a distance, than with a closer *looking through*.

Today, I feel led toward something a bit bolder. Now, when I consider the prospect of gazing at this icon in the manner of prayer, I imagine glimpsing something of the heartache of God—a God who suffers with all of those who are marginalized because of who they are; those whose vocation and ministry is dismissed or curtailed; a God who weeps alongside those whose witness to the truth goes unrecognized or scorned; and who labor under oppressive forces and hostile circumstances.

And I imagine catching a vision, too, of God's slow work of transformation and liberation—a work that might well span decades, persisting through shifting circumstances and massive relocations and uprooting. This slow and steady work of transformation and liberation, summons *our* participation as tellers and hearers of bigger stories—stories made larger by their honest complexity, by a commitment to the truth. A truth that, alone, will set us free.

That, I believe, is what it means to witness in every circumstance to our Savior Jesus Christ, who—for Florence Li Tim-Oi and for us—is always and eternally the Way, the Truth, and the Life.

6

Forgiveness

Forgiveness in the Face of Injustice

Thomas Jay Oord, PhD

Senior Scholar at the Wesley Center for Applied Theology,
Northwest Nazarene University (Sermon delivered September 2015)

In the spring of 2015, I was laid off from my job as a tenured professor of theology. The official reason for my layoff was a dip in enrollment. The real reason was mostly political. I was not afraid to ask big questions and seek believable answers. My doing so in public made me a threat to some in power.

Just about every scholar aware of my ordeal would say my academic freedom was compromised. I went through a theological trial called "an administrative inquiry." Although the result of the trial did not lead to my being considered heretical, my university president asked me to leave. I declined.

In large part because of my being laid off, the faculty met and gave the president a no-confidence vote affirmed by 77 percent of the faculty. The president resigned about a month after that. My layoff, the no-confidence vote, and an "inappropriate relationship" nearly twenty years earlier contributed to his decision to resign.

The majority of university trustees, however, voted to uphold the president's decision to lay me off. This vote surprised my colleagues and me. While the president had not broken the letter of the law when he laid me off, he had broken its spirit. I was a tenured, award-winning professor with more time of service than most of my colleagues and probably the largest publishing record of any professor in the institution. It was clear that I was targeted.

In the midst of my struggle, I endeavored to love no matter what. I consistently reminded myself to live in love despite the injustice. To me, love matters most.

Although my family and I were supported by university faculty and many administrators and staff, we also endured intense emotional and psychological pain. We felt betrayed and abused. We struggled in so many ways, and that pain persists today. As of this sermon, I have not yet found another job.

When trustees decided to uphold the president's layoff decision and I was forced to negotiate a severance, I began to think carefully about what my forgiveness might mean. This sermon represents my thoughts about forgiving the president who laid me off and those trustees who voted to uphold that layoff.

As a Christian theologian, I'm especially interested in what the Christian tradition says about forgiveness. I like to contemplate, for instance, what it means to say God forgives. I also wonder why horrible things happen if God loves everyone and can control anything. For this sermon, I'll set aside the question of why God doesn't prevent evil, because I've addressed it in other books and sermons. Instead, I mostly want to ponder what it means for humans to forgive.

Before getting to what I think forgiveness is, I want to say what forgiveness is not. Forgiveness does not require forgetting. Forgetting may be impossible for many. And sometimes we must remember past evil to inspire us to prevent evil in the future. Forgiveness does not require feeling warm fuzzy feelings. Those who have been hurt may wish to feel positive feelings. But such feelings often take time or never come at all. Forgiveness does not require us to be happy about what happened. Anger toward evil is an important part of being a morally mature person. But we must not allow our anger to become revenge, spite, resentment, or retaliation. Forgiveness does not ask us to be passive. Forgivers are activists.

They have experienced injustice firsthand, and they are choosing to fight it. Forgiveness is not the same as reconciliation. Reconciliation requires all the estranged parties to act positively toward one another, and that may never occur. Forgivers need not wait for the perpetrators of evil to seek reconciliation. Our forgiving does not require perpetrators to ask to be forgiven. We can forgive even if those who harmed us are unaware of their injuring. We can forgive even when those who harm feel justified in their harmful acts.

So far, I've talked mostly about what forgiveness is not. Now let me talk about what it is. As I see it, forgiveness is a form of love. At its core, love involves promoting well-being. It encourages flourishing, positivity, and abundant life. Love advances the efforts of healing, health, and wholeness. Simply put: love does good.

Forgiveness is a form of love that means intentionally acting to do good to those who have harmed us. It usually involves a pardoning statement of some kind and subsequent actions that treat well or wish wellness to those who have treated us poorly. It also typically involves a long road to change negative emotions to positive ones.

Jesus said love does not repay evil with evil. Those who love repay evil with good. That's what forgiveness does: it expresses goodness in response to evil or harm. Incidentally, I define *agape* as a kind of love that promotes well-being in response to actions that promote ill-being. The *agape* form of love does not retaliate against those who have done injury. In other words, *agape* repays evil with good. As I see it, *agape* and forgiveness are closely related. I believe the power to forgive comes from God, whether we believe in deity or not. Just as we love because God first loved us, I think we can forgive because God first forgives us. But some people love and forgive without consciously being aware that their ability to do so comes from God.

In recent days, I have repeatedly asked God to empower me to forgive those who have harmed my family, my colleagues, my friends, and me. I believe that God calls me to forgive in the manner God has forgiven others and me. My forgiving as God forgives allows me to live life to the fullest.

God is in the goodness business. And forgiveness brings the goodness of healing, wholeness, and health—in a variety of ways—to a world of hurt, pain, and suffering. I want to participate in that work.

So, what does it take forgive those who harm us? Often the first step in forgiving is simply deciding to forgive. Deciding to forgive means acting for the good of those who have been bad to us. It means wishing them well in our thoughts and actions. Forgiveness does not seek revenge. It does not harbor bitterness or resentment, but it deals with those negative feelings when they arise. Forgiveness is not vindictive. It consciously chooses to do right to those who have done us wrong. Saying "I forgive" just once is seldom sufficient. Our thoughts and emotions often bring us back to the hurt. We must frequently say "I forgive" to deal with painful thoughts and emotions. I repeatedly decide to forgive. I often say to myself and to others that I forgive those who harm me. Like an athlete who practices her sport so it becomes second nature, I practice forgiveness in the hope that it becomes second nature. Fortunately, the more times we decide to forgive, the more we talk about forgiveness, and when we participate in communities that promote forgiveness, the likelier we will be to choose to forgive when we are hurt. Strong habits of forgiveness make us the kind of people who find forgiveness normal.

Deciding to forgive—in a moment or a long series of instances—is usually accompanied by a second step. This second step is sometimes more difficult and often not entirely within our ability to control. The second step involves transforming our emotions. Transforming our emotions rarely occurs overnight. Transformation takes time. But forgiveness research and various religious and moral traditions teach us to replace the negative emotions with positive emotions of health and healing. Interestingly, those who forgive typically reap greater benefits than the benefits that forgiveness brings to those who harmed them. Forgivers typically have improved physical, psychological, and social/relational health. Unforgiving people live wearisome and anemic lives.

We can deal with negative emotions and thereby have a change of heart when we empathize with the perpetrator of our pain. Empathizing often involves placing ourselves in that person's shoes, thinking about that person's own history and motivations. When we empathize, we see those who have hurt us as broken, insecure, and injured persons themselves. We also try to see the world from their perspective. This helps us understand their motivations a little, without requiring us to justify or condone what they have done. When we empathize with perpetrators of evil, we need not approve or endorse the evils done. We can feel repelled, repulsed, and angry at the pain they have caused. But in empathy, our "hearts go out" to those who have been hurtful. We seek to understand them and their lives in some redemptive way.

The process of empathizing with those who perpetrate evil often involves admitting that we too have harmed others. We have also sinned. We admit that at times in our lives we have caused harm to others. Perhaps our sins have not been as awful as the sins of others. But we also need to be forgiven.

Finally, countless examples suggest that those who forgive well often work to help others. Turning inward and becoming entirely self-focused often leads to depression. But reaching out is a powerful act that helps us and those we help. The old saying, "It is better to give than to receive," has a portion of truth in it. We can and should work toward our own healing. But often the best way to find healing for ourselves is to seek healing for others. In fact, forgiveness most often occurs in community. This community can come from a wise friend or professional counselor. It can come from a small accountability group or caring friendship. Books and other literature can channel this community that encourages forgiveness. At its best, the church is comprised of people who forgive.

In my own situation, I am choosing to forgive. I choose to forgive those who have hurt me, my family, my colleagues, and others. My choice to forgive is one I repeat often. I repeat my commitment to forgive when additional harm is done. I repeat my commitment when hurtful memories invade my mind or negative emotions press upon me. I also try to empathize with those who have hurt others and me. I accept their humanity, complete with its ignorance and limitations. And as I remember the harm I have done, some of the negative emotions I feel toward those who hurt me dissipate. In my forgiving, I also seek to be active. I try to help others who have also been hurt. Forgiveness combats injustice and tries to change structures that do harm. It repays evil with good. To forgive is to love. Among other reasons, I forgive because I want to imitate a forgiving God by living a life of love that resembles the loving life Jesus lived.

I am choosing forgiveness, because I want to live a life of love.